Let's Discover The States

The Southwest

COLORADO • NEW MEXICO • TEXAS

By
Thomas G. Aylesworth
Virginia L. Aylesworth

CHELSEA HOUSE PUBLISHERS
New York   New Haven   Philadelphia

Created and produced by Blackbirch Graphics, Inc.

DESIGN: Richard S. Glassman
PROJECT EDITOR: Bruce S. Glassman
ASSOCIATE EDITOR: Robin Langley Sommer

Printed in Hong Kong

Manufactured by Oceanic Graphic Printing Productions.

Library of Congress Cataloging-in-Publication Data

Aylesworth, Thomas G.
 The Southwest: Texas, New Mexico, Colorado.

 (Let's discover the states)
 Bibliography
 Includes index.
 Summary: Discusses the geographical, historical, and cultural aspects of Texas, New Mexico, and Colorado, using maps, illustrated fact spreads, and other illustrated material to highlight the land, history, and people of each individual state.
 1. Southwest, New—Juvenile literature.   2. Texas—Juvenile literature.   3. New Mexico—Juvenile literature.   4. Colorado—Juvenile literature.   [1. Southwest, New.
2. Texas.   3. New Mexico.   4. Colorado]   I. Aylesworth, Virginia L.   II. Title.
III. Series: Aylesworth, Thomas G. Let's discover the states.
F878.A95   1988   978   87—18292
ISBN 1–55546–562–5

CONTENTS

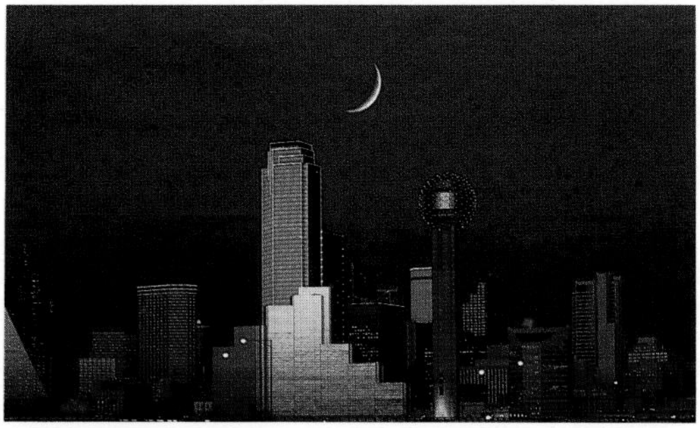

Stark red rocks rising from the Garden of the Gods at
   Colorado Springs.
Skiers sailing down the slopes at Aspen with the wind
   in their ears.
Ancient cliff dwellings in Mesa Verde National Park
   near Cortez.
Watchful marmots near their burrows on the road to
   Pikes Peak.
A sunrise illuminating the grandeur that is Denver
   seen from the mountains.

Let's Discover
Colorado

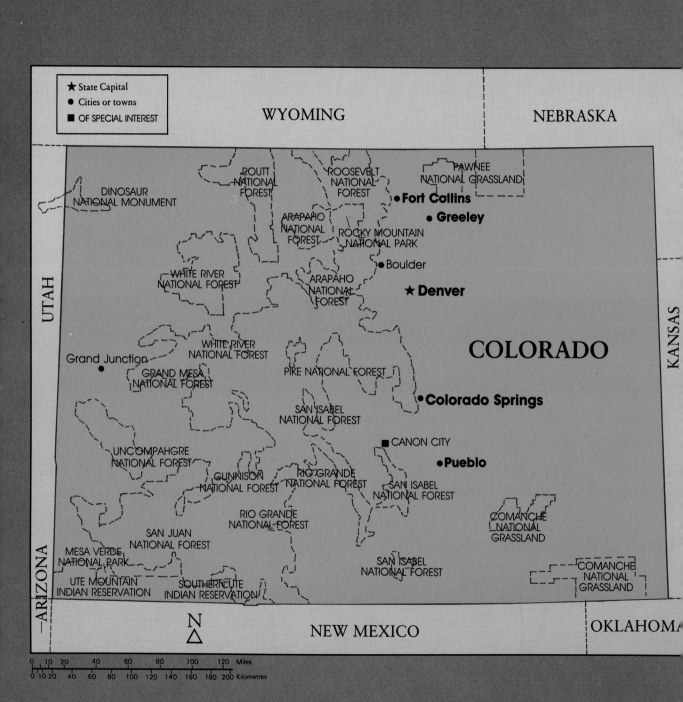

WYOMING

NEBRASKA

UTAH

KANSAS

ARIZONA

OKLAHOMA

NEW MEXICO

COLORADO

DINOSAUR
NATIONAL MONUMENT

ROUTT
NATIONAL
FOREST

ROOSEVELT
NATIONAL
FOREST

PAWNEE
NATIONAL GRASSLAND

● Fort Collins

● Greeley

ARAPAHO
NATIONAL
FOREST

ROCKY MOUNTAIN
NATIONAL PARK

WHITE RIVER
NATIONAL FOREST

● Boulder

ARAPAHO
NATIONAL
FOREST

★ Denver

WHITE RIVER
NATIONAL FOREST

Grand Junction
●

GRAND MESA
NATIONAL FOREST

PIKE NATIONAL FOREST

● Colorado Springs

SAN ISABEL
NATIONAL FOREST

UNCOMPAHGRE
NATIONAL FOREST

■ CANON CITY

● Pueblo

GUNNISON
NATIONAL FOREST

RIO GRANDE
NATIONAL FOREST

SAN ISABEL
NATIONAL FOREST

COMANCHE
NATIONAL
GRASSLAND

RIO GRANDE
NATIONAL FOREST

SAN JUAN
NATIONAL FOREST

MESA VERDE
NATIONAL PARK

SAN ISABEL
NATIONAL FOREST

COMANCHE
NATIONAL
GRASSLAND

UTE MOUNTAIN
INDIAN RESERVATION

SOUTHERN UTE
INDIAN RESERVATION

N
△

0 10 20   40   60   80   100   120   Miles
0 10 20   40   60   80   100 120 140 160 180 200 Kilometres

COLORADO
At a Glance

Capital: Denver

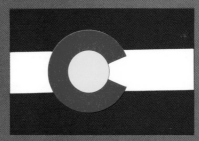
State Flag

State Flower:
Rocky Mountain
Columbine

State Bird:
Lark Bunting

Major Industries: Computer equipment, food processing, aerospace, mining, livestock

Major Crops: Corn, wheat, hay, sugar beets

Size: 104,247 square miles (8th largest)
Population: 3,178,000 (26th largest)

The Land

Colorado is bordered on the west by Utah, on the north by Wyoming and Nebraska, on the east by Nebraska and Kansas, and on the south by New Mexico and Oklahoma. There are four major land regions in the state: the Colorado Plateau, the Intermontane Basin, the Rocky Mountains, and the Great Plains.

The Colorado Plateau lies along most of the western border, from north to south. It covers almost one-fifth of the state, and is a region of high hills, plateaus, deep valleys, and mesas—flat-topped hills with steep sides. The mesas support cattle and sheep ranches, and in the valleys farmers raise fruit, hay, beans, and vegetables. The region is rich in mineral resources, including oil and natural gas, uranium, copper, zinc, lead, and silver.

The Intermontane Basin is north of the Colorado Plateau on the state's northern border. As its name suggests, it lies between two mountainous regions of the Rockies. Forested hills and sagebrush plateaus form the landscape. Sheep ranches dot the plateaus, and oats and beans are raised here. There is also some coal mining.

The Rocky Mountains occupy central Colorado and a small area at the northwest corner of the state. The Colorado Rockies have been called the "Roof of North America," since more than 50 of their peaks rise 14,000 feet or more above sea level. They are the tallest in the entire Rocky Mountain chain, which extends from Alaska to Mexico. This is a region of forests and forest products, with some hay, oat, and vegetable crops. Extensive mining is carried out: lead, copper, tungsten, beryllium, sand, gravel, molybdenum, silver, and gold are found here. The Continental Divide runs through the Colorado Rockies. Streams east of it flow into the Atlantic Ocean, while those west of it run to the Pacific.

The Great Plains cover the eastern two-fifths of the state and are part of the vast interior plain that extends from Canada to Mexico.

The cool waters of Bear Lake lie at the base of Hallett Peak in Colorado's Rocky Mountain National Park.

The 14,143-foot peak of Mt. Sneffels frames the Dallas Valley near Ouray.

The land slopes from east to west to the foothills of the Rocky Mountains. Irrigation has made it possible to farm the region, and to pasture beef and dairy cattle. Crops raised here include sugar beets, potatoes, barley, corn, wheat, hay, rye, and sorghum.

Colorado is the source of more important rivers than any other state. Rivers that rise here include the Arkansas, North and South Platte, Republican, Rio Grande, Colorado, Gunnison, and San Juan. Many lakes are found in the mountains, including Grand Lake, the state's largest natural lake, which covers about 600 acres.

The mountainous western sections of Colorado are generally cooler than the plains. Because of great differences in altitude within short distances, temperatures and weather conditions can change rapidly as one travels through the state. In Colorado, as in Montana, a *chinook*, or warm wind, often blows down the eastern slopes, raising winter temperatures 20 or more degrees Fahrenheit. In the plains, Burlington has an average January temperature of 28 degrees F. and a July average of 74 degrees F. Leadville, in the mountains, has a January average of 18 degrees F., while its July average is 55 degrees F. The state's precipitation is some 15 inches per year, with most rain and snow falling on the western slopes of the mountains.

The History

Cliff dwellings almost a thousand years old at Mesa Verde are all that remains of the Pueblo-type Anasazi culture that flourished in Colorado between A.D. 750 and 1300. By the time Spanish explorers arrived, the region was inhabited primarily by nomadic Plains Indians, including the Arapaho, Cheyenne, Comanche, Kiowa, and Pawnee. The Utes lived in the mountain valleys.

Mesa Verde, in the south-western part of the state, was the home of prehistoric Indians who built elaborate cliff dwellings.

The Spaniards who came to what is now Colorado about 1541 were looking for gold. When they failed to find it, they returned to Mexico, leaving no settlements. In 1682 the French explorer Robert Cavelier, known as La Salle, claimed part of the eastern region for his country when he asserted dominion over the vast territory he called Louisiana. The Spanish returned in 1706, when Juan de Ulibarri claimed the territory for Spain.

Most of present-day Colorado became part of the United States in 1803, with the Louisiana Purchase from France, which sold its territories west of the Mississippi to the young United States. Zebulon M. Pike, an army officer and explorer, entered the Colorado region on a surveying trip in 1806. In his report he described the steep mountain that was named for him—Pikes Peak.

Pike was followed in 1820 by another exploration party under the leadership of army officer Stephen H. Long. Thirteen years later, the first permanent American settlement in the region, Bent's Fort, was set up by the Bent and St. Vrain Fur Company near the present site of La Junta. Kit Carson and other frontiersmen used it as a base.

When Mexico claimed its independence from Spain in 1821, the part of western Colorado that was still under Spanish rule became Mexican territory. The United States and Mexico went to war for title to the Southwest and California in 1846, and a million square miles of territory, including western Colorado, were acquired in 1848, when Mexico was defeated.

When gold was discovered along Cherry Creek in 1858, a stream of prospectors poured into the area that is now Denver. Rich strikes the following year brought fresh wagon trains filled with gold seekers: their slogan was "Pikes Peak or Bust." By the end of 1859, some 100,000 people had come to Colorado. Silver was discovered soon afterward, and additional prospectors arrived. Mining camps, most of them crude tent cities clinging to the rugged slopes of the Rockies, sprang up to become part of Colorado's colorful, robust history.

Newcomers to Colorado ignored both Indian rights to the land and U.S. government treaties that had promised to respect those rights. They set up what they called the Jefferson Territory, which the government refused to recognize. Finally, Congress created the Colorado Territory in 1861, and the U.S. Army waged war on the Colorado Indians for the rest of the decade. In 1864 Colorado militia

Denver, the "Queen City of the Plains," and the capital of the state of Colorado was founded by prospectors in 1859.

ed by Colonel John M. Chivington attacked peaceful Cheyenne and Arapaho villagers at Sand Creek and killed hundreds of men, women, and children in what became known as the Sand Creek Massacre. It was one of the darkest chapters in American history. The United States government admitted responsibility for the tragedy and awarded the Indians some compensation for their losses. In 1868 a large force of Indians attacked 50 U.S. Army scouts near the Arikaree River in eastern Colorado. The resulting battle lasted for days before fresh troops rescued the soldiers.

The Meeker Massacre of 1879 was the last major combat between Indian and government forces in Colorado. Indian agent Nathan C. Meeker, who tried to make small farmers of the Utes on unsuitable reservation land, was killed during an uprising, and the U.S. Army moved in to quell the riot. The venerable Ute chief Ouray intervened to restore order.

Railroads reached Colorado in 1870, when the Denver Pacific linked Denver with the main line of the Union Pacific at Cheyenne, Wyoming. That same year the Kansas Pacific completed a line to Denver, and Colorado was tied to the East Coast. Irrigation systems were developed in eastern Colorado to open the vast plains to profitable agriculture.

Colorado claimed its nickname as the Centennial State when it was admitted to the Union in 1876, just 100 years after the signing of the Declaration of Independence. Territorial governor John L. Routt was elected the first governor of the nation's 38th state.

The discovery of gold in the Rocky Mountains in 1858 brought prospectors and settlers to the Colorado Territory.

In 1893, when business was in a nationwide decline, the federal government cancelled its agreement to buy large quantities of Colorado silver. The mining towns of Leadville and Aspen were severely affected, but Robert Womack's major gold strike at Cripple Creek helped revitalize the mining industry. (Later Leadville was restored as a tourist attraction and Aspen became a popular ski resort.)

In 1902 construction began on the railroad that would cross the mountains to the West Coast, and by 1910 Colorado had almost 800,000 residents. Oil had been discovered in the 1860s, but it did not become a major industry until the automobile was developed at the turn of the century. This new form of transportation also made Colorado a popular vacation and recreation center.

During the 1940s, Colorado's economy and population kept growing. When the United States entered World War II, in 1941, the government established several military bases in the state. Wartime demands for defense and consumer goods kept employment high in the mining and petroleum fields. The postwar selection of Colorado Springs as the site of the new United States Air Force Academy, and installation of major peacetime military bases, brought continued growth. New dams and reservoirs were built, and the Alva B. Adams Tunnel carried water through the mountains to formerly arid eastern farmlands.

Today manufacturing, mining, and tourism all contribute to Colorado's prosperity, and new residents arrive every year, attracted by the beauty and diversity of the "highest state."

The first school in Colorado was established near Denver in 1859 to teach the children of gold miners. By 1862 many other towns had their own public schools. The first public library in Colorado opened in 1860, and a year later the region's first institution of higher education, the University of Colorado, was founded at Boulder. By the time Colorado became a state, four other colleges and universities were operating: the University of Denver (1864), Colorado State University (1870), Colorado College (1874), and the Colorado School of Mines (1874).

The People

More than 80 percent of the people in Colorado live in large towns and cities such as Denver, Colorado Springs, Pueblo, and Boulder. Although most Coloradans are Protestants, the Roman Catholic Church is the largest single religious group. Major Protestant denominations include the Baptist, Methodist, Presbyterian, and United Church of Christ.

Heavyweight champion Jack Dempsey, born in Manassa, Colorado, works out at Stillman's Gym in New York, in 1920.

Astronaut Scott Carpenter, a native of Boulder, speaks to President Kennedy after his successful orbital flight in 1962.

One of the best-known people from Colorado is Byron R. "Whizzer" White. This All-American football player for the University of Colorado went on to play professional football with the Pittsburgh Pirates (now the Steelers) and the Detroit Lions, and was elected to the Pro Football Hall of Fame in 1954. Today he is a justice of the United States Supreme Court. White was born in Fort Collins.

M. Scott Carpenter, the pioneering astronaut who completed a three-orbit space-flight mission in 1962, was a native of Boulder. In the field of sports, Jack Dempsey, heavyweight boxing champion of the world from 1919 to 1926, came from Manassa. Paul Whiteman, who helped popularize jazz with his internationally famous orchestra, was born in Denver, and Ralph Edwards, the radio and television personality, came from Merino. Well-known actors from Colorado include Douglas Fairbanks, Sr., Pat Hingle, and Jan-Michael Vincent, all from Denver; Ken Curtis of Lamar; and Denver Pyle of Bethune.

The United States Air Force Academy

OF SPECIAL INTEREST

NEAR COLORADO SPRINGS: *The United States Air Force Academy*
The "West Point of the Air" opened in 1958 to train the nation's Air Force
officers; its strikingly modern Cadet Chapel is unique.

NEAR CANON CITY: *Royal Gorge*
This massive canyon cut by the Arkansas River is crossed by the world's highest
suspension bridge.

IN DENVER: *Larimer Square*
A restoration of the first street in Denver, the square contains Victorian shops,
galleries, and restaurants.

NEAR ESTES PARK: *Roosevelt National Forest*
More than 780,000 acres of lakes, streams, and beautiful mountain scenery almost
surround the town of Estes Park.

NEAR CORTEZ: *Mesa Verde National Park*
Ancient cliff dwellings with ceremonial pits called kivas recall the pueblo culture
that began with the Anasazi, or Old Ones.

For more information write:
DENVER AND COLORADO CONVENTION & VISITORS BUREAU
225 WEST COLFAX AVENUE
DENVER, COLORADO 80203

FURTHER READING

Abbott, Carl. *Colorado: A History of the Centennial State*. Colorado Associated
University Press, 1976.
Carpenter, Allan. *Colorado*, rev. ed. Childrens Press, 1978.
Casewit, Curits W. *Colorado*. Viking, 1973.
Downey, Matthew T., and Metcalf, F. T. *Colorado: Crossroads of the West*.
Pruett, 1976.
Fradin, Dennis B. *Colorado in Words and Pictures*. Childrens Press, 1980.
Sprague, Marshall. *Colorado: A Bicentennial History*. Norton, 1976.

The pageantry and color of a ceremonial Indian dance
  at the San Ildefonso Pueblo.
Bats whirring out from the Carlsbad Caverns at
  sundown.
Mesas rising from the desert valley north of Gallup.
The sights, sounds, and smells of Old Town in
  Albuquerque.
Sunlight gleaming from the stark white gypsum sands
  at White Sands National Monument.
The serenity of the ancient pueblo ruins in the
  Coronado State Monument near Bernalillo.

Let's Discover

New Mexico

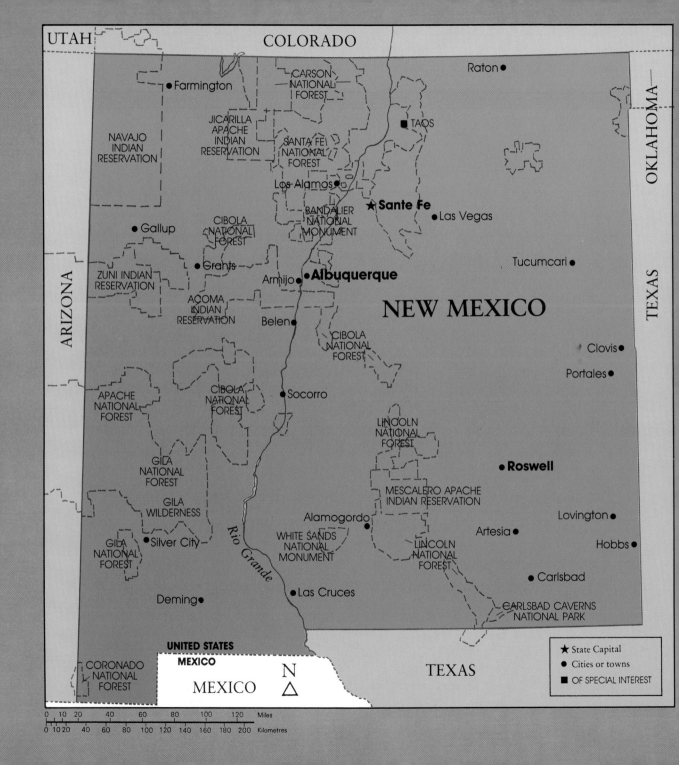

UTAH
COLORADO
OKLAHOMA

• Raton

• Farmington

CARSON
NATIONAL
FOREST

JICARILLA
APACHE
INDIAN
RESERVATION

NAVAJO
INDIAN
RESERVATION

SANTA FE
NATIONAL
FOREST

■ TAOS

Los Alamos•

BANDALIER
NATIONAL
MONUMENT

★ **Sante Fe**

• Las Vegas

ARIZONA

• Gallup

CIBOLA
NATIONAL
FOREST

• Grants

Armijo• • **Albuquerque**

NEW MEXICO

• Tucumcari

ZUNI INDIAN
RESERVATION

ACOMA
INDIAN
RESERVATION

Belen•

CIBOLA
NATIONAL
FOREST

✦ Clovis•

Portales•

APACHE
NATIONAL
FOREST

CIBOLA
NATIONAL
FOREST

• Socorro

LINCOLN
NATIONAL
FOREST

GILA
NATIONAL
FOREST

• **Roswell**

MESCALERO APACHE
INDIAN RESERVATION

GILA
WILDERNESS

Alamogordo•

• Lovington

GILA
NATIONAL
FOREST

•Silver City

WHITE SANDS
NATIONAL
MONUMENT

Artesia•

LINCOLN
NATIONAL
FOREST

Hobbs•

Rio Grande

•Carlsbad

Deming•

•Las Cruces

CARLSBAD CAVERNS
NATIONAL PARK

UNITED STATES

MEXICO

N

CORONADO
NATIONAL
FOREST

MEXICO

△

TEXAS

★	State Capital
●	Cities or towns
■	OF SPECIAL INTEREST

TEXAS

0	10	20	40	60	80	100	120	Miles

| 0 | 10 | 20 | 40 | 60 | 80 | 100 | 120 | 140 | 160 | 180 | 200 | Kilometres |

NEW MEXICO

At a Glance

Capital: Santa Fe

State Flower: Yucca

Major Crops: Wheat, hay, sorghum, cotton

Major Industries: Electrical machinery, agriculture, mining

State Bird: Roadrunner

State Flag

Size: 121,666 square miles (5th largest)

Population: 1,424,000 (37th largest)

25

The Land

New Mexico is bordered on the west by Arizona, on the north by Colorado, on the east by Oklahoma and Texas, and on the south by Texas and the Mexican states of Sonora and Chihuahua. The state has four main land regions: the Great Plains, the Rocky Mountains, the Basin and Range Region, and the Colorado Plateau.

The Great Plains cover the eastern one-third of New Mexico and are part of the vast plain that extends from Canada to Mexico. Many deep canyons have been cut by streams in the area to the west, where cattle and sheep are raised. Corn, wheat, peanuts, and cotton are grown here, and oil and natural gas are pumped from the ground.

Chaco Canyon, in northwestern New Mexico, is a national monument preserving many ancient Indian dwellings.

The Rocky Mountains of New Mexico are in the north-central area and extend south almost to Santa Fe. In this region the Rio Grande (Great River) cuts between the main mountain ranges. East of the river is the Sangre de Cristo Range, which includes Wheeler Peak; at 13,160 feet above sea level, it is the highest point in the state. West of the river are the Nacimiento and Jemez Ranges. Oil, natural gas, and coal are found here, and some fruit and forest products are produced.

The Basin and Range Region extends south and west from the Rockies to the borders of Mexico and Arizona, covering about one-third of the state. This is an area of scattered mountain ranges, between which are basins—low places where streams have no outlet. Mines in the region produce gold, iron ore, copper, lead, zinc, and silver. There are numerous cattle ranches, and poultry, Angora goat, and sheep farms. Irrigation also allows fruits, vegetables, pecans, and cotton to be raised.

The Colorado Plateau is in northwestern New Mexico. This is a land of wide valleys and plains, deep canyons, sharp cliffs, and rugged mesas—flat-topped hills. To the south are badlands, made up of extinct volcanoes and arid lava plains. Uranium, coal, natural gas,

The Rocky Mountains of New Mexico are a popular attraction for campers and climbers.

and oil are found here, and vegetables, and grains are the chief crops.

The most important river in New Mexico is the Rio Grande, which runs from north to south through the center of the state. Several large dams along the river form reservoirs for storage of irrigation water, which is essential to agriculture in most of the state. The Pecos, San Juan, Canadian, and Gila are other important New Mexican rivers whose waters are used for irrigation.

Dry air and warm temperatures are typical of New Mexico, where readings of 75 degrees Fahrenheit prevail in July. In winter, the north averages 35 degrees F. and the south, 55 degrees F. Only about 20 inches of rain and snow fall yearly, most of the snow in the northern mountains.

The History

People have lived in New Mexico for some 20,000 years. Ten-thousand-year-old projectile points and other artifacts discovered near Folsom, in northeastern New Mexico, indicate that Paleo-Indians hunted and lived in the region. From approximately 500 B.C. to A.D. 1200, the Mogollon people lived in the valleys along the New Mexico-Arizona border. These early farmers constructed circular huts, with earth and wood roofs covering storage pits, usually in the shadow of overhanging cliffs. Later they built rectangular above-ground multi-room houses. In northwestern New Mexico were the Anasazi, who developed a high form of civilization. They raised corn, beans, gourds, and cotton, and tamed wild turkeys, which were part of their diet. In the winter, the turkey feathers provided warm robes. The Anasazi and their descendants were cliff dwellers, who built many-storied apartment houses of adobe (sun-dried clay) using masonry techniques. One of them, at Chaco Canyon, extended over three acres and had more than 800 rooms. Before A.D. 1500, the nomadic Navaho settled near the Pueblo Indians and learned to raise corn and to weave cotton. The Navaho learned to raise sheep from the Spaniards, and wove the wool into spectacular rugs and blankets. From Mexicans they learned to make jewelry of silver and turquoise. The Apache and others used horses that had escaped from the Spaniards to pursue buffalo and lived in huts or tipis as they followed the herds and other game.

The Spaniards arrived in what is now New Mexico by accident. In 1528 an exploring party sent to seek gold in Florida was shipwrecked near the Texas coast. About 80 survivors, led by Álvar Núñez (known as Cabeza de Vaca), were captured by Indians and forced to work for them. Cabeza de Vaca and three shipmates finally escaped and made their way across Texas to the Rio Grande and thence to Mexico (New Spain). Their reports of rich Indian cities to the north led to further expeditions in search of these "Seven Cities of Cibola," which soon became legend.

In 1539 a Franciscan monk named Marcos de Niza set out to explore the territory, guided by one of the survivors of the shipwreck, an African slave named Estévan. De Niza arrived in what is now New Mexico in May of that year. From a nearby mesa, he viewed the Zuñi pueblo of Hawikuh, not far from present-day Gallup. But his guide was killed there, and he returned to Mexico after claiming the region for Spain.

De Niza's report so impressed the viceroy that in 1540 he sent Francisco Vásquez de Coronado and his army, with de Niza as guide, to explore what is now New Mexico and Arizona. The party searched for two years, but found no gold; The Indian pueblos did not have the wealth of the fabled Seven Cities. Coronado returned home in 1542 a disappointed man. In 1581 the region was explored by the monk Augustín Rodríguez and a soldier named Francisco Sánchez Chamuscado, who traveled up the Rio Grande from

Acoma, an Indian village about 50 miles west of Alberquerque, was established about 1100 A.D. This makes it the oldest, continuously occupied site in the United States.

The monks who accompanied the Spanish explorers founded missions throughout the territory of New Spain.

Mexico. Their report, and that of the explorer Antonio de Espejo, persuaded the Spanish government to colonize New Mexico.

Don Juan de Oñate established the first Spanish settlement in New Mexico in 1598: the Pueblo of San Juan de Los Caballeros, near the Chama River. He was the first governor of the province. In 1610 his successor, Pedro de Peralta, moved the provincial capital to Santa Fe, which makes this city the oldest seat of government in the United States.

Roman Catholic missionaries set up schools to teach Christianity to the Indians, whom the civil authorities mistreated. As in Mexico, they were forced to do heavy labor and punished for worshipping their ancestral gods. By 1680 there were Spanish villages all along the Rio Grande. Then the Pueblo Indians, led by Popé, rebelled with Apache help and drove every colonist and missionary form New Mexico. More than 400 Spaniards were killed in the Pueblo Revolt.

But the Indians lacked a central government, and in 1692 Don Diego de Vargas, the Spanish governor, reconquered the province with little difficulty. For the next 125 years, Spanish colonists and Pueblo Indians co-existed uneasily.

New problems arose in the early 1800s, when American trappers and traders came into New Mexico. Spanish officials were determined to maintain control at any price, even that of forbidding trade with their nearest neighbors. They expelled the Americans, or put them into prison.

When Mexico threw off Spanish rule in 1821, New Mexico became part of the new empire to the south. William Becknell of Missouri brought the first wagons across the trackless plains and blazed what would become the Santa Fe Trail. As American settlers pushed farther west during the next 25 years, tensions grew between the United States and Mexico, resulting in the Mexican War of 1846. New Mexico became a United States Territory in 1850, two years after the war ended in an American victory. The original New Mexico Territory included what is now Arizona and part of present-day Colorado. The territory was enlarged on the south by the

Gadsden Purchase of 1853. The present boundaries of New Mexico were established in 1863, after Congress created the territories of Colorado and Arizona.

Confederate troops from Texas captured much of New Mexico, including Albuquerque and Santa Fe, early in the Civil War. But Union forces soon regained the region after two battles near Santa Fe—at Apache Canyon and Glorieta Pass. From 1862 to 1864, Colonel Kit Carson led the New Mexicans in a war that forced the Mescalero Apache and the Navaho onto reservations.

During the late 1870s, the Lincoln County War broke out when cattlemen and other factions vied for political control of the county. The murder of rancher John C. Tunstall touched off widespread violence in which "Billy the Kid" Bonney and other outlaws played a major part. In 1878 General Lewis "Lew" Wallace was appointed territorial governor and restored order by declaring martial law.

When the railroads arrived in the 1880s, New Mexico experienced rapid growth. The cattle industry flourished with access to distant markets, and settlers arrived from all parts of the country. Fear of the Apache Indians, who had long resisted American encroachment on their territory, diminished as most members of the tribe were confined to reservations. In 1885 the great Chiricahua Apache chief Geronimo (Goyathlay) fled from an Arizona reservation with some of his warriors and terrified settlers with raids from his base in Mexico. But when Geronimo and his band surrendered to General Nelson A. Miles in 1886, the Apache Wars were over.

In 1912 New Mexico became the 47th state, with a population of some 330,000. The mining of copper, silver, and other mineral resources had become a thriving industry, although farming and ranching remained important. In 1916 the Mexican revolutionary Francisco "Pancho" Villa and his men raided Columbus, New Mexico, and killed 17 Americans. General John J. Pershing crossed the Mexican border, but failed to find Villa in the northern mountains. A year later, the United States entered World War I, and more than 17,000 New Mexicans served in the armed forces.

One of the legendary outlaws of New Mexico was William H. Bonney, better known as Billy the Kid (1859–1881).

The narrow gauge railroads equipped with steam engines brought settlers to New Mexico. They are now a popular tourist attraction.

A prolonged drought in the 1920s hurt the farming and ranching industries of New Mexico a decade before the nation suffered through the Great Depression of the 1930s. When livestock prices dropped, many banks closed and ranchers were forced into bankruptcy. The economy revived with the discovery of oil and the mining of huge potash deposits in the Carlsbad area.

In 1941 a New Mexico regiment, the 200th Coast Artillery, was stationed in the Philippines when the Japanese attacked Pearl Harbor and the United States entered World War II. The 200th and other American forces were overwhelmed by Japanese troops on the Bataan Peninsula, and those who were not killed spent more than three years in Japanese prison camps under intolerable conditions. During the war, the U.S. government established the town and laboratory of Los Alamos to develop the atomic bomb, which was first exploded in a test near Alamogordo on July 16, 1945. Within weeks the bomb was dropped on the Japanese cities of Hiroshima and Nagasaki, with devastating results. Survivors are still being treated for the effects of radiation more than 40 years after the surrender of Japan.

In the postwar period, New Mexico has enlarged its role as a scientific research center, especially in the field of atomic power. Rocket and missile research has been conducted at White Sands since 1945, and uranium, a component in nuclear fuels and weapons, was discovered in the state in 1950. Tourism has grown rapidly since the vast caverns at Carlsbad became a national park in 1930. Santa Fe and Taos are vital centers for the arts and attract many visitors. Industries like oil and uranium now yield more than $6 billion per year.

Education in New Mexico goes back to the early 1600s, when Spanish missionaries started schools for the Indians. Archbishop Jean Baptiste Lamy founded the region's first permanent school, in Santa Fe, in 1853. The first library had opened there two years earlier. St. Michael's College, established in 1859, was New Mexico's first institution of higher education, and five others were founded before the turn of the century: New Mexico State University (1888), the University of New Mexico (1889), New Mexico Institute of Mining and Technology (1889), New Mexico Highlands University (1893), and New Mexico Western University (1893).

One of the nation's most innovative and well-known undergraduate institutions, Saint Johns College, is located in Santa Fe, with a sister campus in Annapolis, Maryland.

Indian dances and ceremonies are still performed near the *pueblos* (indian villages) of New Mexico.

The People

About 72 percent of the people of New Mexico live in towns and cities such as Albuquerque, Roswell, and Santa Fe. Most New Mexicans are descendants of the Indians and of the Spanish- and English-speaking people who settled the area. About 98 percent of them were born in the United States. The majority of New Mexicans are Protestants, including Baptists, Episcopalians, Methodists, and Presbyterians. Roman Catholics make up the state's largest single religious community.

Famous New Mexicans include Archbishop Jean Baptiste Lamy, who spent most of his life as a missionary teaching and working among the poor after he arrived from France in the mid-1800s. His career was immortalized by novelist Willa Cather in *Death Comes for the Archbishop*. Artist Georgia O'Keeffe, born in Sun Prairie, Wisconsin, moved to the flourishing artists' and writers' colony at Taos in 1929 and became famous for her stark, simple paintings of natural forms, such as *Yellow Cactus Flower*.

Artist Georgia O'Keeffe (1887–1986) lived in the artists' colony in Taos, and painted numerous landscapes of the stark New Mexico desert.

Cartoonist Bill Mauldin, born in Mountain Park, became a hero to American soldiers of World War II for his realistic depictions of the average G.I.s "Willie and Joe" in the military newspaper *Stars and Stripes*. Mauldin returned from the war to become one of our most respected political cartoonists. New Mexico's contributions to the stage and screen include actress Kim Stanley, born in Tularosa, and silent-film actress Mae Marsh, a native of Madrid.

Carlsbad Caverns

OF SPECIAL INTEREST

NEAR CARLSBAD: *Carlsbad Caverns National Park*
This series of huge limestone caves contains fantastic rock formations and a
    chamber 4,000 feet long. Visitors gather to see great clouds of bats fly out at
    dusk to feed on insects.

NEAR SANTA FE: *Bandelier National Monument*
The ruins of four ancient Indian pueblos can be viewed here at one of New
    Mexico's nine national monuments.

IN ALBUQUERQUE: *Old Town*
Located on the site of the original settlement, made in 1706, this district has a
    charming Spanish flavor and interesting shops and restaurants.

IN SANTA FE: *Palace of the Governors*
Built in 1610, this adobe construction is the oldest public building in the United
    States. It now houses an historical museum.

NEAR TAOS: *La Hacienda de Don Antonio Severino Martinez*
This early Spanish hacienda, or large estate, was also used as a fortress during
    Indian raids.

For more information write:
THE TRAVEL DIVISION
NEW MEXICO COMMERCE & INDUSTRY DEPARTMENT
BATAAN BUILDING
SANTA FE, NEW MEXICO 87503

FURTHER READING

Beck, Warren A. *New Mexico: A History of Four Centuries*. University of
    Oklahoma Press, 1982.
Carpenter, Allan. *New Mexico*, rev. ed. Childrens Press, 1978.
Fradin, Dennis B. *New Mexico in Words and Pictures*. Childrens Press, 1981.
Jenkins, Myra E., and Schroeder, A. H. *A Brief History of New Mexico*. University
    of New Mexico Press, 1981.
Reeve, Frank D., and Cleaveland, A. A. *New Mexico: Land of Many Cultures*, rev.
    ed. Pruett, 1980.
Simmons, Marc. *New Mexico: A Bicentennial History*. Norton, 1977.

The low, gray chapel called the Alamo standing amid
the tall buildings of downtown San Antonio.
The beauty of the mountains, deserts, and lakes of the
Big Bend country.
Oil rigs rising from the Great Plains, sharing the
landscape with vast herds of cattle.
Thousands of red-clad fans yelling "Hook 'em,
Horns!" on a Saturday afternoon in Austin's
Memorial Stadium.
The drama of the Guadalupe Mountains—the ancient
reef of a vanished sea.

Let's Discover
Texas

TEXAS
At a Glance

Capital: Austin

Major Industries: Machinery, transportation equipment, petroleum, livestock

Major Crops: Cotton, grain, fruits, nuts

State Bird: Mockingbird

State Flower:
Bluebonnet

Size: 267,338 square miles (2nd largest)

Population: 15,969,000 (3rd largest)

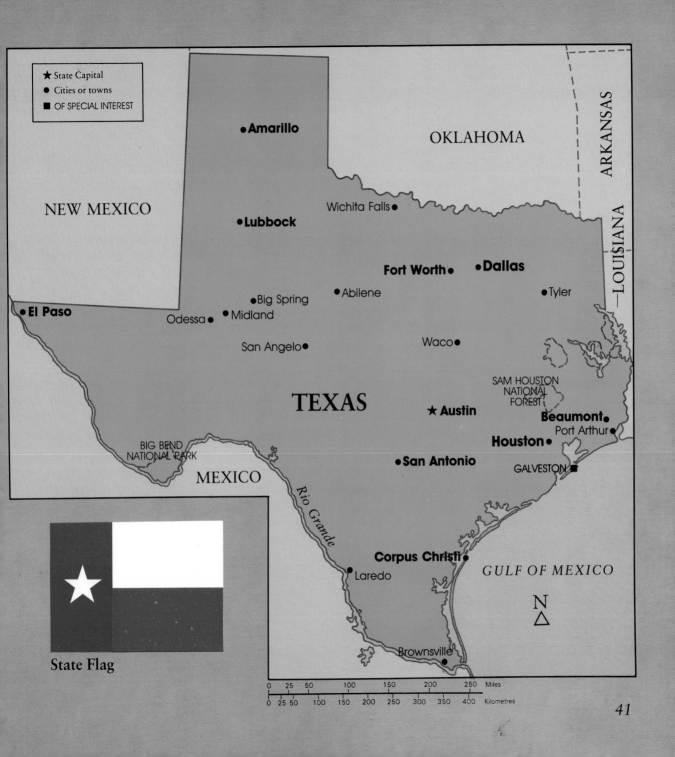

★ State Capital
● Cities or towns
■ OF SPECIAL INTEREST

NEW MEXICO

●Amarillo

OKLAHOMA

ARKANSAS

LOUISIANA

Wichita Falls ●

●Lubbock

Fort Worth ● ●Dallas

●Big Spring ●Abilene ●Tyler

●El Paso Odessa● ●Midland

San Angelo● Waco●

TEXAS

SAM HOUSTON
NATIONAL
FOREST

★ Austin Beaumont●
Port Arthur●

Houston●

BIG BEND
NATIONAL PARK

MEXICO ●San Antonio

GALVESTON ■

Rio Grande

Corpus Christi●

GULF OF MEXICO

Laredo●

N
△

Brownsville●

| 0 | 25 | 50 | 100 | 150 | 200 | 250 | Miles |
| 0 | 25 50 | 100 | 150 | 200 | 250 | 300 | 350 | 400 | Kilometres |

State Flag

The Land

Texas is bordered on the west by New Mexico and the Mexican state of Chihuahua, on the north by Oklahoma and Arkansas, on the east by Arkansas and Louisiana, and on the south by the Gulf of Mexico and the Mexican states of Tamaulipas, Nuevo Leon, and Coahuila. Texas has four main land regions: the West Gulf Coastal Plain, the North-Central Plains, the Great Plains, and the Basin and Range Region.

The West Gulf Coastal Plain is a strip of land from 150 to 300 miles wide along the Gulf Coast; it is part of a larger area that stretches from Texas to Florida. The shorelands of the warm Gulf of Mexico include subtropical regions and fertile areas that specialize in winter vegetables and fruits. Commercial fishermen ply the waters of the Gulf for shrimp, sea trout, and red snapper. Timber and wood products are important industries, and cattle are pastured on huge ranches. Large deposits of coal, natural gas, oil, salt, and sulfur are also found in the region.

The North-Central Plains, which form a huge thumb-shaped area in the north-central part of the state, have the largest population and some of the best farmland in Texas. Thick grasses make this an ideal region for cattle raising. Cotton, grains, fruit, and pecans are grown, and numerous wells produce oil and natural gas.

The Great Plains extend south from the western half of the Panhandle to the lower part the state. The altitude here ranges from about 700 feet above sea level to more than 4,000 feet in the west. The region has vast wheat farms and the richest petroleum and natural gas fields in the country. Building stone and salt are quarried here, and there are many cattle, goat, and sheep ranches.

The Basin and Range Region is also called the Trans-Pecos. It is the southern extension of the Rocky Mountains: a land of high, dry plains in the far western part of the state. Livestock and pecans are among the region's agricultural products.

Davis Mountain State Park in west Texas is a popular place for hiking and nature study.

Corpus Christi, on the Gulf of Mexico, is the ninth largest port in the country. Pleasure craft as well as many fishermen anchor here.

Tourists admire the waterfalls at Lake Buchanan, a highlight of the Vanishing Texas River Cruise.

The coastline of Texas along the Gulf of Mexico measures 367 miles. But if the shorelines of the bays, offshore islands, and rivermouths are included, it stretches for 3,359 miles. The major river is the Rio Grande, which forms the southern border, between Texas and Mexico. Other important rivers are the Pecos, Colorado, Guadalupe, Neches, Nueces, Brazos, Red, Sabine, San Antonio, and Trinity.

   The climate of Texas varies widely from one end of the state to the other, with the coldest readings found in the northern Panhandle. There January temperatures average 35 degrees Fahrenheit, with a 76-degree-F. average in July. In southern Texas, warm, damp weather with temperatures of 60 degrees F. in January and 85 degrees F. in July is the norm. Eastern Texas has up to 46 inches of precipitation per year, while western Texas averages only 8 inches or less. Strong winds accompanied by sleet and rain can sweep across the state in winter, but snowfall occurs only in the north.

Horseback riding in Big Bend National Park, in the curve of the Rio Grande, brings visitors in direct contact with the desert lands of the American Southwest.

The History

Spanish conquistadors, commanded by Francisco Coronado, explored Texas in the 16th century, while searching for the famed Seven Cities of Cibola.

When the Spaniards arrived in what would become Texas in the 1500s, some 30,000 Indians were living in the region. In the east were the Caddo—farmers who lived in permanent dwellings. Some of them, including the Nacogdoches, Nasoni, and Neche tribes, formed a league called the Hasinai Confederacy. Along the coast were the Arkokisa, Attacapa, Katankawa, and other small tribes. Some of the Indians of Coahuila lived in the southern part of the region, adjacent to Mexico. In the plateaus to the west were the nomadic Lipan Apaches, and the north-central plains were hunting grounds for the Comanche and Tonkawa.

Just 27 years after Columbus discovered America, the Spanish began to explore Texas in the name of "glory, God, and gold"— mainly gold. In 1519 Alonzo Álvarez de Piñeda, who sailed from Jamaica, began to explore the Gulf Coast from Florida to Mexico, mapping it as he went. In 1528 another Spanish expedition was shipwrecked on the Texas coast. There were four survivors, one of whom, Álvar Núñez (called Cabeza de Vaca), led his companions on a trek among the Indians that lasted eight years and ended at a Spanish settlement near the Pacific Coast of New Spain (Mexico). There they told stories about Indian cities of great wealth in what is now the American Southwest.

Inspired by these tales, Francisco Vásques de Coronado set off from Mexico in 1540 to look for the Seven Cities of Cibola—those fictitious realms of gold. With him was a Roman Catholic priest, Fray Juan de Padilla, the first Franciscan missionary to the region, who was later killed by the Indians whom he was trying to convert. The group passed through Texas in 1541 and reached the adobe dwellings of the Pueblo Indians farther west, but found no gold. Disappointed, Coronado gave up the search in 1542.

Hernando de Soto, the Spanish governor of Cuba, ventured from the west coast of Florida to what is now Oklahoma beginning in

1539. He died on the expedition, but some of his men pushed on into northeast Texas, reaching the vicinity of what is now Texarkana in 1542. Spain claimed the Texas area as a result of these explorations, and two missions were established by the Franciscans in 1682 near what is now El Paso.

The French entered the region in 1685, when Robert Cavelier (called La Salle) landed at Matagorda Bay and established a colony named Fort Saint Louis. This settlement was destroyed by the Indians two years later. But Spain was alarmed by the French presence, and sent new explorers and missionaries to strengthen its hold on the area. In 1690 a Franciscan friar traveling with the expedition of Alonso de León established the first mission in east Texas, San Francisco de los Tejas, along the Neches River.

By 1731 the Spanish had sent more than 90 expeditions into Texas. Many missions and forts were established, including the fort of San Antonio de Bexar, which was built to protect the mission of San Antonio de Valero. The settlement became the city of San Antonio. It was the seat of Spanish government in Texas from 1772 onward. Texas grew slowly because of its size and remoteness from Mexico City. More than 100 years after Spanish colonization began, the region had only about 7,000 settlers.

When the United States completed the Louisiana Purchase from France in 1803, it claimed that portion of Texas to which France had taken title during the 1600s. In 1819 the Adams-Onis Treaty with Spain gave the United States the rights only to a point bounded by the Sabine and Red Rivers.

When Mexico won its freedom from Spain in 1821, Texas was a part of the short-lived Empire of Mexico. Three years later Mexico became a republic, with Texas and Coahuila as one of its states. In 1820 a Missouri banker, Moses Austin, had asked Mexican officials to let him set up an American colony in Texas. The request was approved, but Austin died before he could organize the colony on the Brazos River. His son, Stephen F. Austin, brought 300 American families to Texas in 1821, and they established settlements at Washington-on-the-Brazos and Columbus, in southeastern Texas. In

1823 Austin laid out the settlement of San Felipe de Austin, in present-day Austin County, as the colonial seat of government. Mexico gave Austin additional land grants, and he expanded the boundaries of his colony.

Other Americans moved into Texas with the permission of the Mexican government; by 1830 Texas had a population of 25,000 settlers, most of them from the United States. But the Mexican government had become alarmed by the number of Americans in Texas, and conflict developed. In 1830 Mexico forbade further American immigration into Texas and the importation of slaves.

Mexican general Antonio López de Santa Anna became dictator-president of Mexico in 1833. He abolished the federal constitution and demanded personal control of state governments. In 1835 the American colonists in Texas revolted against Mexico. They had several battles with Mexican troops before their leaders met at San Felipe de Austin to organize a temporary government. The Texans formed a small army, and troops led by Colonel Benjamin Milam attacked San Antonio, taking control of the town on December 11, 1835. Santa Anna rushed north to put down the revolt with a large Mexican army. At San Antonio, a handful of American Texans, outnumbered 30 to 1, retreated into an old mission, the Alamo, to make a stand. Santa Anna's attack on the Alamo lasted from February 23 to March 6, 1836. The American garrison fought to the last man. All of the defenders, including Jim Bowie, Davy Crockett, and William B. Travis, were killed.

With the cry "Remember the Alamo!" Texas leaders met at Washington-on-the-Brazos and declared Texas independent of Mexico. David G. Burnet was chosen temporary president of the Republic of Texas, and Samuel Houston was made commander of the army. Santa Anna was still trying to put down the revolution. He had some 330 Texas prisoners shot to death in the town of Goliad, but the Texans continued to fight. In April 1836, Houston and his small army took Santa Anna's large army by surprise in the Battle of San Jacinto, defeating the superior force and capturing Santa Anna.

The best known historical site in Texas is the Alamo, the mission in San Antonio where a small force of 187 Texans was besieged by a large Mexican army in 1836.

Above:
Jim Bowie (1796–1836), a settler from Georgia, commanded the garrison at the Alamo. He invented the Bowie knife, a popular weapon used on the Western frontier.

At right:
The defenders of the Alamo included a former congressman from Tennessee, the frontiersman Davy Crockett (1786–1836), seen at right being bayoneted by a Mexican soldier.

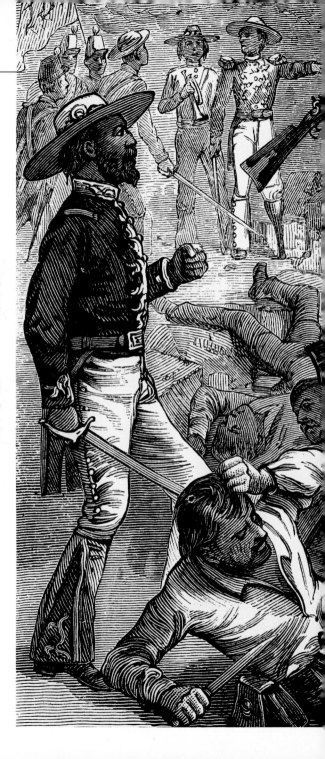

This victory ended the war and raised the republican flag, with its single star, over what would become the Lone Star State.

Sam Houston became the new president of the Republic of Texas, but many problems remained. The government had little money available, and parties of Mexicans continued sporadic raiding from across the disputed southern border. The obvious answer was to petition the United States for annexation, which the Republic did. However, European nations, especially France and Great Britain, wanted Texas to be independent so that the United States would not gain control of the Southwest. The Southern states wanted Texas in the Union because it was a slave-holding territory, but the North opposed the idea for the same reason. The Republic of Texas was not admitted to the Union for 10 years. In 1845 it became the 28th state.

When Texas was admitted to the Union, Mexico broke off diplomatic relations with the United States. Long-standing disputes over the Rio Grande border between Texas and Mexico were a major cause of the Mexican War, which began in 1846. Mexico surrendered in 1848, and gave up its claims to Texas, New Mexico, and California in the Treaty of Guadalupe Hidalgo.

Texas left the Union to join the Confederacy when the Civil War began in 1861. But the decision was not unanimous. Governor Samuel Houston, who had worked for union with the United States since 1838, refused to take an oath to support the Confederate States of America. He was put out of office and retired from public life.

More than 50,000 Texans fought for the Confederacy during the war, and the state sent huge quantities of food, textiles, and other goods to support the Southern cause. The Texas coast was blockaded by the Union Navy, which also occupied Galveston for a time. Although the Civil War ended on April 9, 1865, its last battle was fought on May 13 at Palmito Ranch, near the mouth of the Rio Grande, by soldiers who had not heard that the war was over.

The Reconstruction era that followed the Civil War brought occupation by federal troops and widespread racial violence incited by the Ku Klux Klan. After Texas was readmitted to the Union in

Sam Houston (1793–1863)
commanded the Texans at the
Battle of San Jacinto and later
became the president of the
Republic of Texas.

Galveston, which lies on a low island off the Gulf Coast, still contains many elaborate houses such as the Bishop's Palace, built in 1886.

1870, conflict decreased, and many new settlers moved in. Cattle ranching became a major industry, and large farmlands opened up along the railroad lines that crossed the state in the 1880s. Richard King extended the 75,000-acre tract he had bought in 1853 into the world's largest ranch—the 1.27-million-acre King Ranch, with some 40,000 cattle.

In 1900 a devastating hurricane struck the island city of Galveston, in the Gulf of Mexico, and killed some 6,000 residents in one of North America's worst natural disasters. The city was rebuilt into a major port for dry-cargo shipping. A year later, discovery of the Spindletop oil field near Beaumont signaled a new role for Texas as one of the nation's leading producers of oil and natural gas. Refineries and manufacturing plants were built, and coastal harbors were deepened to accommodate large ships that transported oil to world markets. When the United States entered World War I in 1917, many military training camps opened in the state.

In 1925 Texas became the second state, after Wyoming, to have a woman governor. She was Mrs. Miriam A. "Ma" Ferguson, who ran for office after her husband, Governor James E. Ferguson, was impeached. She was later elected to a second term.

During World War II, about 1,250,000 members of the armed forces trained in Texas. In 1947 the state suffered another major disaster when a French ship loaded with chemicals blew up in the harbor at Texas City. About 500 people were killed, 3,000 were injured, and the loss in property was about $70 million.

Today Texas is still expanding its industries, with emphasis on cotton products such as clothing, machinery, and processed foods. The state has become a major center for both space research and construction, which is now a multi-billion-dollar business. Oil has long been vital to the state's economy, but the petroleum industry has been hurt by declining prices in the mid-1980s, especially in the Houston area.

Franciscan friars opened the first schools in Texas during the 1600s to teach farming techniques, spinning, and weaving to the

Indians. During the period of Mexican rule, the government refused to set up schools with English-speaking teachers. But in 1854, nine years after statehood, a public-school system was established. The first library was organized in Austin by the Republic of Texas in 1839. Southwestern University (1840) was the first institution of higher education. When Texas became a state, there were two more—Mary Hardin-Baylor College and Baylor University, both

Houston is a major port for oil tankers, which reach the inland city by the 50-mile Ship Channel.

Once the center of the Texas cattle industry, Houston has grown to a major city since the discovery of oil.

founded in 1845. By the turn of the century, Texas had 24 colleges and universities, including Austin College (1849), Saint Mary's University of San Antonio (1852), Trinity University (1869), Texas Agricultural & Mechanical University (1871), Texas Christian University (1873), Sam Houston State Teachers College (1879), The University of Texas (1881), Rice University (1891), Our Lady of the Lake College (1896), and Southwest Texas State College (1899).

The NASA Lyndon B. Johnson Space Center near Houston has played a major part in the space program since the Mercury flights in the early 1960s. It is now the center of the shuttle program.

Mariachi bands, a tradition brought from Mexico, stroll along the Paseo del Rio in San Antonio.

The People

Almost 80 percent of the people in Texas live in towns and cities such as Houston, Dallas, San Antonio, Fort Worth, El Paso, Austin, and Corpus Christi. About 97 percent of them were born in the United States, and most of those who were born in foreign countries came from Mexico. The largest single religious group is the Roman Catholic. Other important denominations are the Baptists, Methodists, members of the Churches of Christ, Disciples of Christ, Presbyterians, and Episcopalians.

Two of America's 20th-century presidents have come from Texas. Dwight D. Eisenhower, the 34th president, who commanded Allied armies in World War II before his first election, was born in Denison. Lyndon B. Johnson, the 36th president, whose social-reform program called for "the Great Society," grew up near Stonewall.

Texas military men of renown besides Eisenhower include Admiral Chester W. Nimitz, a naval commander of World War II, who was born in Fredericksburg, and Audie Murphy, the most decorated American soldier of that war, a native of Farmsville.

Billionaire industrialist, aviator, and moviemaker Howard Hughes came from Houston. Writer Katherine Anne Porter, best known for the novel *Ship of Fools*, was born in Indian Creek.

Below left:
The descendants of the German farmers who settled Fredericksburg in the 1840s celebrate Founder's Day.

Below:
The Tigua Indians, the oldest ethnic community in Texas, live on a Reservation near El Paso.

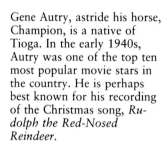

Gene Autry, astride his horse, Champion, is a native of Tioga. In the early 1940s, Autry was one of the top ten most popular movie stars in the country. He is perhaps best known for his recording of the Christmas song, *Rudolph the Red-Nosed Reindeer*.

Texas has also produced many luminaries in the field of entertainment. Joshua Logan, the Broadway producer-director responsible for such hits as *Mister Roberts* and *South Pacific*, was born in Texarkana. Dancers from Texas include Cyd Charisse (Amarillo), Ann Miller (Houston), and Alvin Ailey (Rogers). Broadway stars from the Lone Star State include Mary Martin (Weatherford) and Debbie Allen (Houston), and popular singers make up an impressive list: Janice Joplin (Port Arthur), Gene Autry (Tioga), Mac Davis (Lubbock), Jimmy Dean (Plainview), Kris Kristofferson (Brownsville), Barbara Mandrell (Houston), Roger Miller (Fort Worth), Kenny Rogers (Houston), and Tina Turner (Brownsville).

Film and television personalities from Texas include Academy Award-winner F. Murray Abraham (El Paso), Steve Martin (Waco), Valerie Perrine (Galveston), Dennis and Randy Quaid (Houston), Debbie Reynolds (El Paso), Sissy Spacek (Quitman), JoBeth Williams (Houston), Carol Burnett (San Antonio), and Larry Hagman (Fort Worth).

Vice President Lyndon B. Johnson (1905–1973) became the president following the assassination of President Kennedy in 1963. He retired to his ranch on the Pedernales River at the end of his second term.

The San Jacinto Monument

OF SPECIAL INTEREST

IN SAN ANTONIO: *The Alamo*
This famous chapel in downtown San Antonio was besieged by a great Mexican
   army in 1836 and defended to the last man by Americans committed to the
   independence of Texas.

NEAR HOUSTON: *San Jacinto Monument*
This 570-foot monument, the tallest structure of its kind, commemorates the Battle
   of San Jacinto, in which Texas won its independence from Mexico.

IN AUSTIN: *Daughters of the Republic of Texas Museum*
The museum houses relics of pioneer life in the Republic of Texas during the
   mid-1800s.

IN WESTERN TEXAS: *Big Bend National Park*
The Rio Grande, the looming Chisos Mountains, and a vast desert extending north
   from Mexico form a landscape of unforgettable beauty in the last great
   wilderness area of Texas.

IN GALVESTON: *Bishop's Palace*
This architectural masterpiece, built in 1886, has magnificent examples of marble,
   mosaic, carving, and stained glass.

For more information write:
CHAMBER OF COMMERCE
1012 PERRY-BROOKS BUILDING
AUSTIN, TEXAS 78701

FURTHER READING

Carpenter, Allan. *Texas*, rev. ed. Childrens Press, 1979.
Connor, Seymour V. *Texas: A History*. AHM, 1971.
Fehrenbach, Theodore R. *Lone Star: A History of Texas and the Texans*.
   Macmillan, 1968.
Fradin, Dennis B. *Texas in Words and Pictures*. Childrens Press, 1981.
Frantz, J. B. *Texas: A Bicentennial History*. Norton, 1976.
Richardson, Rupert N., and others. *Texas: The Lone Star State*, 4th ed. Prentice-
   Hall, 1981.

INDEX

Numbers in italics refer to illustrations

Photo Credits/Acknowledgments

Photos on pages 5, 6–7, Jeff Gnass; pages 11, 12, Ron Ruhoff, Colorado Tourism Board; pages 13, 22–23, 26, 30, Jill Heisler; pages 14–15, New York Public Library; pages 8, 16, 31, 46, 49, 50, 51, Culver; pages 19, 35, 60, Wide World; page 20, U.S. Air Force; pages 21, 25, 27, 29, 32, 34, 36, Mark Nohl, New Mexico Department of Economic Development and Tourism; pages 37, Texas Tourist Agency, page 40 (right), 58 (right), Michael Murphy, pages 43, 45, 54, 56, 57, 59, 62, Richard Reynolds; page 44, O.C. Garza; pages 38–39, 42, Tourism Division, Texas Department of Commerce, pages 53, 61, National Portrait Gallery.

Cover photograph courtesy of Tourism Division Texas Department of Tourism.

The Publisher would like to thank Richard Reynolds of the Texas Department of Commerce, Tourism Division, and the staff of the Colorado and New Mexico Departments of Travel and Tourism for their gracious assistance in the preparation of this book.